Miraculous Journey

Words Manifested from Beyond the Veil

Bernadette O'Neill

BALBOA
PRESS

A DIVISION OF HAY HOUSE

This book is a work of non-fiction. Unless otherwise noted, the author and the publisher make no explicit guarantees as to the accuracy of the information contained in this book and in some cases, names of people and places have been altered to protect their privacy.

Balboa Press books may be ordered through booksellers or by contacting:

Balboa Press
A Division of Hay House
1663 Liberty Drive
Bloomington, IN 47403
www.balboapress.com
1 (877) 407-4847

Because of the dynamic nature of the Internet, any web addresses or links contained in this book may have changed since publication and may no longer be valid. The views expressed in this work are solely those of the author and do not necessarily reflect the views of the publisher, and the publisher hereby disclaims any responsibility for them.

The author of this book does not dispense medical advice or prescribe the use of any technique as a form of treatment for physical, emotional, or medical problems without the advice of a physician, either directly or indirectly. The intent of the author is only to offer information of a general nature to help you in your quest for emotional and spiritual well-being. In the event you use any of the information in this book for yourself, which is your constitutional right, the author and the publisher assume no responsibility for your actions.

Any people depicted in stock imagery provided by Getty Images are models, and such images are being used for illustrative purposes only.
Certain stock imagery © Getty Images.

Print information available on the last page.

ISBN: 978-1-9822-2247-5 (sc)
ISBN: 978-1-9822-2248-2 (hc)
ISBN: 978-1-9822-2252-9 (e)

Library of Congress Control Number: 2019902052

Balboa Press rev. date: 04/05/2019

Dedication

For my daughters; Alexa and Megan, my grandchildren; Dallas, DreVonte, Dominique, and Luna, may you always have the courage to speak your truth with love and light; and to my dear sister, Peggy —beyond the veil- until we meet again.

Acknowledgement

Thank you to Aimee, Roxanne, Cindy, Kate, Bill and Pam for listening to my words as they arrived, and to my family; Theresa, my mother, Douglas, my father, Michelle, my sister, Danny, my brother-in-law, Aunt Kay and Uncle Kenny, and to Joe, my husband—thank you for loving me. I send my love and sincere gratitude to each of you for your encouragement and assistance.

Dear Reader,

I want to thank you for reading my poems and allowing me to share my journey with you. If you enjoy them and they help you in some way, please consider giving a copy of my poems to someone you know, to help me spread my message of love and light, forgiveness and healing, on my journey back to Self. I pray that my words help you on your personal journey.

Sincerely,

Bernadette O'Neill

Just B

Contents

Gifts

Dear Spirit
As you shine your light
Upon my path
I step upon it quick and fast

All my gifts
You give to me
To make my life
As it should be

Health, happiness
Prosperity
Spiritual enlightenment
Are there for me

Thank you Dear Spirit
For letting me see
All that life
Is offering me

Just B

The Poet

I am a poet
I just did not know it
Until I was standing there

The words started flowing
Without my own knowing
The message I had to share

But as I looked down
At the words that I found
All I could do is just stare

The messages found
Oh how profound
I hope all who read them will care

Just B

Just Be

When I am done
With day's brilliant light
And settle myself down
With the darkness of night

I find all the answers
Within my own head
To lead me on forward
To my journey ahead

This journey is special
I know not where it leads
So for now I will wonder
I will feel, I'll Just Be

Just B

Inspiration

Early morn
Just out of the shower
That is the time
My finest hour

Words from beyond
They come to me
Just the way
They are meant to be

Now on the run
Words have begun
They now appear
Out of thin air

Inspiration
Sweet mystery
I love the way
You come to me

Just B

Journey Forward

One step at a time
The path will unfold
We journey forward
To places untold

Where we are heading
The mystery revealed
Is part of our journey
To places yet sealed

So keep moving forward
One day at a time
To all of the places
Awakened inside

Just B

Obsession

My magnificent obsession
Has taken my lifetime to conceive
It has crept up from behind me
All around me, deep inside me

My creation taken form
I myself could not truly see
It mystified me and defied me
But still it crept up deep inside me

As I go about my days
Taking care of details on the way
My creation it has found me
Moving forward, out around me

As I accept that in my essence
There is a special kind of presence
My creation starts to lead me
It overtakes me to release me

Just B

The Darkness

The darkness is insidious
It can creep up slow or fast
It shows up in many different forms
It always seems to last

Listen to that tingling
That feeling when you ask
What snuggled up inside of me?
Your heart will beat so fast

What is that deep down nagging?
That makes you feel so blue
It can show up dressed as anger
Or when you're crying too

Watch out for negativity
It also likes to play
It shows up unexpectedly
And wants to stay all day

Protect your precious energy
When you do you'll see
The special kind of person
That you are meant to be

Just B

Gift from the Goddess

Dear Goddess of beauty
Strength and light
You guide me through
Both day and night

You shine your light
For me to see
A glimpse upon
My destiny

Sweet gift from you
My words appear
They take away
My inner fear

Just B

Messenger

You can grow old
Or be Divine
Was the wise woman's
Message to me

She said that Goddesses
Surround me
What a revelation
That be!

My dream that night
Did confirm it
The black birds
Delivered to me

Message was sent
From the Great Goddess
Wake up
And be set free

Just B

Forward Movement

Are you afraid
Of what goes bump in the night?
Does the unknown
Make you shiver with fright?

Take a deep breath
And clear out your head
Take a good look
Then move on ahead

Move to the left or
Move to the right
Keep going straight or
Move backwards, you might

The decision is yours
Which way you will go
Whatever you choose
It will help you to grow

Release inhibitions
And all of your fears
You will feel free
For all of your years

Just B

Goddess

The way to manifest
Lies deeply within
The magic unfolding
Is yet to begin

The life I have lived
Up to this day
Has been put before me
To pave my new way

As I learn all the magic
This world has to hold
I will master new gifts
As I connect to the old

I have lived this already
But I cannot recall
What I shared with my sisters
Still my craft will unfold

Oh The Wise Mother,
Maiden, Sacred Crone
You have guided me here
I have been not alone

Just B

Oh Goddess, the keeper
Where all secrets are found
Your Magical Moon Phases
We will join in the round

We ask the Gatekeepers
Of all secrets unknown
From North, East, South, and West
We must move in the round

In our circle we open our hearts up to you
Oh Great Goddess
Protect us
We give all up to you

Just B

Earth Guides

People come and people go
Some are meant to stay
Others come to teach us things
To learn along the way

I think about who's come and gone
What we've done along the way
Some things were great, some not so good
All lessons to pave the way

Just B

Star Seed

She said I'm an Indigo
What does that mean?
The message I'm holding
I have not yet seen

Indigo aura
I am a Star Seed
From out in the universe
How do I heed?

Who do I look to?
What do I do?
To reach my own insight
And give it to you

I wander, I journey
Toward my next phase
To pass on the message
I'm meant to engage

This message within me
I struggle to find
Will come to me soon
All in good time

Just B

Day by Day

Little intergalactic traveler
Sent down here from afar
Deliverer of messages
I know not what they are

Stranger among the many
Going day by day
Watching for my little clues
That will guide me on my way

Where is it that I'm going?
Who will I meet along the way?
Time will tell throughout my life
As I take it day by day

Star actor in this play called life
Learning my script along the way
Waiting for my lines, Divine
I will shape them come what may

Just B

Ascended Masters

Healing words I've received
Gifted to me
Sent from The Masters
Here before me

Ascension they mastered
From our great land
Their energy heals me
Here as I stand

As I receive healing
I flourish and grow
I'm here to help others
So they too can grow

Beautiful Masters
I thank you so much
For your precious gifts
With them I do much

Just B

Lost in Plain Sight

As I sit here today
No obstacles in my way
I reflect on the return of my sight

I think back to the past
How could it all last?
The loss of all I could do

Now reflecting today
I feel ready to play
The role that I'm here to live

What it's meant to be
Still my big mystery
Day by day it will come back to me

All the things I can do
Will return to the light
They're no longer lost in plain sight

Just B

Guiding Light

I am ready to stand
Here in my power
It's always scared me
Until this hour

I now embrace it
I no longer erase
The guiding light
Inside of me

Now that it's here
I plan to share
With others
My gift of sight

Show them the way
So they can stay
Directly in
Their light

Just B

New Path Unfolding

Cryptic messages
Now unfold
From deep within
My soul

But alas
I must go
The day's begun
No time for fun

Get up, get ready
To work I go
My current path
It's real

But words still come
The process begun
My new path
It's revealed

Just B

The Universal Cup

Early morn
The sun's not up
My words arrive from
The Universal Cup

My minds awaking
Words pouring forth
They're here now
Just for the taking

Another message
It's coming in
Back I go
To paper and pen

Record them now
As they arrive
Words with me now
They are alive

The message here
It is now clear
Grab it fast
It will not last

Just B

Memory Lane

A walk in the park
I choose Memory Lane
As I think of all
That has been

I step onto the path
Relaxing at last
All my memories
Start trickling in

A bird starts to sing
Precious song for today
I recall
All that has once been

Autumn's leaves all around
The wind rustles the sound
One great rush
Brings them all to the ground

Just B

Interference Overcome

Don't engage
What you do not know
Don't interact
Don't let it grow

Words of protection
Said out of fear
All "for the best"
Did interfere

What changed in fact
What I could have been
But don't reflect on
What was back then

The path once taken
Was destined to be
To shape and mold
What is inside of me

The real journey
Is here and now
To share and to guide
Others somehow

Just B

Times Gone By

Penny candies
Remember when?
Would you do it
All again?

Off to church
Each Sunday
That is where
I learned to pray

Girl school stint dressed in a "gimp"
Blue socks to knees
White, pressed blouse
If you please

Memories bring me
Back again
To times gone by
Remember when?

Just B.

Alone

Sweet little girl
So gentle and shy
What was the reason?
Who's to say why?

Always surrounded
In the big crowd
But all by yourself
Like no one's around

Who could you turn to?
What could you do?
Time is the healer
It came here for you

Learning to know
What you're all about
Now nothing can stop you
You've let yourself out

Just B

The Big Picture

Be a good girl
Do as I say
All of my life
This was the way

But here at last
I look at the past
What can I say?
It's my turn to play

Writing, drawing
Numbers I see
They have released
My creativity

At last I accept
Just who I am
There is a big picture
I'm part of The Plan

Just B

No Remorse

Why do you do
The things you do?
I planned on spending
My life with you

But things don't always
Turn out as planned
Life sometimes slips
Right through our hands

But when I reflect on
What could be
I see life is where
It is supposed to be

No remorse
I could not stay
Not back then
And not today

Just B

Early Departure

Once there were three
Until that day
The word received
You went away

Pain and anguish
Filled your space
Oh how I long
To see your face

Sister Dear
The third in line
Will we meet again
In time?

Not just now
We must somehow
Live without
Your grace

Just B

Spirit Guide

Dear Spirit
I thank you every day
For always being there
For showing me the way

You shine your light before me
As I walk through my day
Always there to find me
When I go astray

You gently redirect me
Back onto my course
You keep my attention
You are my guiding force

Just B

The Blindfold

The blindfold's off
I now can see
It's always been
In front of me

The games were played
The dice were cast
The plots were formed
Were made to last

But when you choose
A different view
The patterns change
In front of you

The obstacles
That once were there
They rearrange
And disappear

It all can change
It's up to you
With blindfold off
Dreams do come true

Just B

Stepping Out

Come forth dear child
It's time for you
To show the others
What to do

It's time for you
To take a stand
So others will see
And understand

Your points of view
Will come to you
When you step out
Into plain view

Just B

Shawl's Warmth

There has been a sadness
Deep within me, I know
I have carried it with me
Like a shawl around my soul

It has been the insulation
That has kept me safe and warm
Deep within its blanket
My sadness it was born

My illusion of security
Has kept me in my place
Preventing me from growing
From running in the race

Just B

Bright Light

Subdue your excitement
So others can't see
They don't understand it
Or want it to be

Don't shine your light brightly
For others to share
They will only slight you
They'll stop and stare

Compromises you make
To the true you
Will extinguish your light
Of what you can do

Just B

Little Girl

Little Miss Realist
So serious and true
Let your "little girl" come out
From deep inside of you

She's waiting there
So patiently
She wants
To come and play

So let her out
From deep within
Maybe you'll
Let her stay

Just B

Unplanned Words

I can`t plan
What I should write
When I try
It`s never right

My thoughts confuse
They start to fight
I get confused
And lose my sight

Inspiration
Out of thin air
It appears
It is just there

I write it down
It now has form
Inspiration
Comes from my storm

Oh my gosh!
They`re here again
Write them down
Find paper and pen

Just B

Deep Well

Drink from the fountain
The well is deep
Knowledge is there
For you to keep

One sip will bring you
Back again
To drink from it
Your head will spin

Knowledge from
The universal cup
It's there for you
Drink it up

What you will find
Unique to you
Direction there
Specific to you

One sip of knowledge
Is all it takes
For you to see
What you create

Just B

Personal Growth

Are my words meant just for me?
Or are they here for others to see?
Do they hold messages there?
Rays of light with treasures rare

I do not know which way to go
Let them out for others to see?
Or keep them here
Just for me

Share them now
Let others know
How I have found
My way to grow

Just B

Looking Back

When you look at others
And see what they do
And ask yourself
Why not me too?

Look again
And understand
Your decisions and actions
Are creating your plan

Let your life form
Just let it all be
Stop and look back
What do you see?

The life you build
Unique to you
Will take its form
It's all up to you

Just B

Integrity

Do you walk in your integrity?
Do you know it when you do?
It is a special kind of something
That is particular to you

Does that thing that you are doing
Make you sing and want to dance?
Does it make you really happy?
Make you want to take a chance?

While I have walked along my journey
Trying to figure what to do
My little, special kind of something
It has shown me what to do

Sometimes I have listened
Sometimes not so much
One thing is quite certain
It has all meant so much

Just B

In the Flow

Inspiration happens
When it wants to
Just relax and
Let it be

It will happen
When it's supposed to
When it is
Meant to be

In the shower
Out in traffic
Late at night
Or early morn

When it comes
You must release it
Just let it flow
It must be born

Just B

Right Time

All will be
As it is meant to be
All will simply
Flow to me

I have willed it all
To land
It is here
Right in my hand

The time is here
It has begun
It's time to shine
My word is spun

What will become
I still can't see
I have faith
I'll let it be

Just B

Belief

I carry it with me
Wherever I go
You may not see it
You probably don't know

It's silent and secret
My own little plan
I work on it daily
So it soon will land

It's forming and building
Creating its steam
It's leading me onward
To my treasures and dreams

Belief is so powerful
Keep it within you
Give it some space
To show you what to do

Just B

One Step at a Time

Just be who
You truly are
Life will flow to you
You'll be your own star

One step at a time
That's how you will make
Life's constant decisions
Some finished and some late

Commitment and work
For sure it will take
Tomorrow's advancement
I know you will make

Just B

Special Purpose

Everything I do
Everyone I meet
Everywhere I go
Are like pebbles beneath my feet

Each special situation
I have encountered along my way
Creates my special path
On which I am meant to stay

My life has created
The path which I am on
To find my special purpose
To continue bravely on

As I trust my intuition
How can I go wrong?
It is my special purpose
That will help me carry on

Just B

43

Inner Guidance

Listen, can you hear your voice deep within?
It's whispering, it's guiding
And nurturing too
Showing you where to be begin

The next step you take
Towards the true you
Will always be right
And show you what to do

Be quiet and listen
Go deep within
The message you hear
Will guide you through fear

Just B

Happiness

Love and light
Forgiveness
And healing
This is where to begin

To release hurt and pain
Deep inside
And live your life
Once again

Your freedom within
That is where to begin
To live your life
Full of dreams

Enjoy each day
Come what may
Happiness
Finally begins

Just B

Beautiful World

When you start your day
With love leading the way
All of the world's beauty
Will greet you

You won't have to search
With doubt and despair
It will be waiting
For you everywhere

From morning to night
You will not have to fight
Happiness will fill up
Your day

Think of love first
Your heart it will burst
And everyone around you
Will play

Just B

Beautiful You

Beauty is in
The eyes of the beholder
Do you see
Your unique beauty?

See it, release it
It will come back to you
Your true magnificence
Belongs just to you

Love yourself first
And others will see
All of your gifts and
Your inner beauty

Just B

Belief

Do you truly believe
Beyond a shadow of a doubt
In a universe full of love
Full of kindness and giving?

Look at the beauty
In all that you see
It is there to be found
When you truly believe

Trust in the bounty
That is waiting out there
For you to receive
When you truly believe

Raise your vibration
Through belief without doubt
Be amazed at the gifts you receive
When you truly believe

Just B

Intense One

Little Miss Intensity
It comes from deep within
Everything I see I feel
Not knowing where to begin

Sometimes big sometimes small
As it flows into my life
My gifts are here to mend me now
And make me whole again

Little Miss Intensity
So deep and so profound
Take a look around you now
At the beauty you have found

Just B

Destiny

Come to me
My Destiny
My pure
And sweet success

I will have
The things I need
All that is
My inner best

I have waited
Many years
To feel
My sweet success

The hour is now
To feel my power
Success
Without the stress

Just B

Divine Timing

Things don't happen
In my timing
As I wish they would

They happen
In Divine timing
Exactly as they should

I might not get
Just what I want
Because I wish I could

I absolutely get
What I need
To make me well and good

Just B

Freedom Within

Blue skies
Dark clouds rolling in
Look at you
You're back again

Not for me
I have changed
My mind is clear
Bright and free

You can too
Look within
A brand new attitude
It's all new again

I changed my mind
For the rest of time
What manifests
Is truly mine

Just B

Opportunity Knocks

Where were you on the day
When inspiration came to play?
Did you see it as your gift?
There to embrace and bring you bliss

Open up and let it flow
You cannot know where it will go
The new life that it creates
Will free your spirit to a new place

Where all you need
Will wait for you
You will then know
What you should do

When opportunity knocks
At your door
Let it in
There will be more

Just B

Light Workers

Please join me, my friends
As I walk down my path
If it is your intention
To heal from your past

Places I'm going
Revealed as I tread
Experiences coming
I no longer dread

Please join me each day
As I move through my life
Discovering my treasures
To share with my friends

Things that we share
Each day as we go
We help each other
To continue to grow

Bringing light to our world
As we go day to day
Helping others to evolve
To enjoy every day

Just B

Beauty and Splendor

Thank you Dear Spirit
For letting me see
For shining a light
On who I want to be

Releasing my past
All gone at long last
I move forward in light
To achieve and to fight

For the power of good
And a love so profound
You will fall to your knees
At what you have found

The beauty and splendor
In each given day
Is here for the taking
To create what you may

Just B

Inner Glow

Don't judge me as you see me
Come closer, take a second look
I am but a reflection
Of something deep in you

I have my own pure beauty
But it's found way deep inside
Not out there on the surface
Will you find what's truly mine

It is my inner glory
That makes my beauty shine
Not that which stands out on my face
But what bubbles in my mind

You see what's on the surface
Please don't stop at that
I am but a reflection
Of something you might lack

So please take a deeper look at me
When you stop to judge me so
For when you take another look
You will feel my inner glow

Just B

Confusion

So confused and oh so lost
Completely drained within
Looking outward for solitude
The mind begins to spin

Man-made help; the pill, the drink
Leaves you empty within
Forced to settle back inside
The healing then begins

Listen for the voice that comes
From deep within your soul
It will carry you back to ``Self``
For you to then be whole

Just B

Beautiful Irony

Beautiful irony
Stares me in my face
As I sit here
Contemplating my past

All my decisions
I made way back when
I was so young
Would I do it again?

Things I have done
Have shaped
Who I have become
Sitting here writing these words

Bravery it takes
To look my past
In the face
And share it for others to see

I am unique
And so too are you
What can you give
To help others truly live?

Just B

Guiding Light

Days of my past
When I lived hard and so fast
Land of despair I found everywhere
Hiding my light from within

Running from me
From anyone who could see
The part of my Self
That could not be felt

My past party land
Has found me again
Way of the Light
It is shining so bright

Thanks be to You
For guiding me through
My self-made
Pain and despair

Reiki Master at last
And teacher, soon too
I will help others
As guided by you

Just B

Stumbles and Falls

When you stumble
And you fall
Do you get back up
Or do you crawl?

The falls we make
Along our way
They pave the path
So we can play

The roles that we
Are meant to be
Let them come
And you will see

The magic you
Are here to do
It will show up
It's up to you

Just B

Choices

My back to the wall
Move forward
Don't fall

One step at a time
The prize
Will be mine

Move forward to what?
I know not,
But I must

Release doubt and fear
What is meant
Will be there

One at a time
The choices
Are mine

To make as I go
Step by step
I will grow

Stand Tall

Here I am now
My back to the wall
With all I have written
I must stand here tall

Do I move forward
With what I've been given?
Or fall on my knees
Shrunken, not driven?

Choices to make
Which ones do I take?
To move into my power
Within the right hour

I move down my path
To the magical place
With gifts in my hands
To find my own space

Just B.

Dark Night of the Soul

My sight is improving
I can now see
All of the gifts
Deep inside of me

With confidence growing
My clarity of sight
To light my way
Through my dark night

Dark Night of the Soul
It has allowed me to grow
Out of my shell
That place I knew well

Oh what a sight
The brilliant daylight
It has shone down on me
On my creativity

Just B

Golden Thread

Just breath
Just let it be
Tomorrow's light will surely come
To shine it's might; it will be done

Release your pain
Your struggle and strife
All that has followed you
Throughout your life

Release it now
And you will see
The person that you
Are meant to be

It is our challenges
All that we dread
That soon become
Our Golden Thread

It binds us to
Our destiny
To that which we
Are meant to be

Just B

The Voice Within

The power to manifest lies from within
The mystery about it is where to begin?
Energy, Energy, Energy abounds
When you release it, the beauty is found

I lie awake wondering, where do I start?
I talk to my Goddess all around the clock
But when I listen alone late at night
The answers await me in the daylight

I scramble to find my pencil – a pen
To write down my messages - that's where to begin
The mystery to manifest lies deep inside
When you listen to the voice you just can't hide

Just B

Who am I?

A little haggard
Somewhat torn
But I'm still standing
Here in my storm

It's my creation
Each little bit
The joy the heartache
It's been my making

It all has created
Who I am now
I'll change my life
And move forward somehow

Just B

The Universe Within

The Universe is within us
It is but our soul
It molds and it shapes us
As we grow from the old

What road will it take us
To choices we make
They keep moving within us
Till we must forsake

All that no longer serves us
We move steadfastly on
To the path that's before us
And to all that's our own

Just B

Secrets

Seductive secrets
Now being told
The true power
That I hold

What I request
It will be had
Now I see
This power in me

Gift's late arrival
Guaranteed to me
More than mere survival
My success will be

My purpose here
It's taking form
Like nature's fury
In a storm

The tempest now
Is in my hand
Now I see
I understand

Just B

Magical You

Crawl out of the darkness
And into the light
To find your own magic
Your own inner light

Whatever you find
It's all up to you
The barriers and strengths
Intrinsic to you

Step forth from the darkness
Release your own pain
To see what you're made of
To be whole again

Just B

Destination

All is good
It's all aligned
You will arrive
It's right on time

What needs to change
Will be undone
You will get there
And have great fun

When finally there
You will see
How it is all
Supposed to be

Your destination
Waits for you
Then you will see
What's meant to be

Just B

Reciprocity

Happiness has eluded me
All the days of my life
I decided to live
With struggle and strife

I created the trouble
I survived to this day
Now I create my own joy
It is mine come what may

I'm now free of what held me
From creating within
My own form of beauty
Around me again

My life is now full
Of great prosperity
And I give of it all
As guided, I now see

When we give what we have
No agendas to hold
Others to us like magnets
Without their control

Just B

Those who take from my treasures
Must give back once again
To others who need it
It starts over again

Just B

Love

When we start our day
With love leading the way
What wondrous things
Will start to display

From morning to night
As we go round and round
Life's amazing treasures
Are soon to be found

What once was a challenge
To us in the night
Is now nothing but
A bump in daylight

I know this as truth
As I go day to day
Travelling along
My own personal highway

I find on my path
All I need in this life
Without any trouble
Struggle or strife

Just B

So whatever you meet
As you go through your day
You receive all with ease
With Love leading the way

Just B

2018

2018
The energy shift
Shining down
On all

Take time
Be still
It will reveal
Something inside us all

So quiet now
Let it come
Release in you
Your secrets too

What you will see
It's just for you
So be alert
It's coming through

Just B

The Seed

I am the keeper
Of my personal cell
I hold the key
To make it all well

With key in the lock
I turn it to see
All of my answers
Come flowing to me

Special gifts I was born with
They all will appear
When I take my first step
Out into the air

Accept my own powers
I am here at last
To grow and to flourish
To share all, to ask

What do you hold
That another might need?
Look deep inside
Pass on the seed

Just B

Limitations

With my back to the wall
I stood proud
I stood tall
Protected from making a fall

Now I've stepped on my path
And what great surprise
Light shines down so bright
That there's no end in sight

The Plan will unfold
I will take firm control
And behold
I will know what to do

When my wall held me there
In my darkness and fear
Self-limitations
Were all I could hear

Just B

Ground and Centre

Calm down, relax
No need to fret
You're soon to arrive
But not quite yet

The world speeds by
All its affairs
Find comfort and solace
Don't hold their tears

Breathe deeply – centre
You're almost there
Let the world spin by
Your dream soon will be here

Just B

My Tribe

I await the day
That I am joined with my Tribe
Working together
Towards whatever we strive

Learning together
And sharing our gifts
Enlightening others
With laughter and bliss

Experiencing life
With each other is rare
Magical moments
That we long to share

To strengthen the circle
Of friends that converge
We lighten the burden
Of toil and we learn

Our journey upon
This amazing fair plain
This existence is only
The precursor to fame

Just B

As we move gracefully forward
Revealing the gems
That we each bring together
To achieve other realms

Higher moments of bliss
Await all who dare share
All of their personal treasures
Together is rare

But when this reality
Comes into play
What reveals is a beautiful
A wonderful day

Just B

Hidden Key

My Twelfth House full of mysteries
Kept hidden from me
It has taken my lifetime
To find my own key

To release all the treasures
That lie deep within
To help me move forward
And enjoy life again

My gems from past lifetimes
When I was so much more
Are there as my guideposts
To release even more

Of my own special secrets
That lie deep within
When I hear and accept them
My life will begin

When my memories come calling
It is me who will ask
How do I move forward
And be whole at last?

Just B

My Twelfth House full of secrets
I now know where to begin
To tap into past lifetimes
Once deeply hidden

Just B

Twelfth House of Secrets

My Twelfth House of secrets
So elusive and true
You hold the secrets
Of what I can do

Reveal to me
That which you hold
Release the secrets
Yet to be told

Past lives of mine
When I have led
Where other mortals
Have feared to tread

What I could do
In days of old
Oh the stories
That are yet untold

My Twelfth House of Secrets
So dark and taboo
Reveal to me now
What I am to do

Just B

Oh my Dark House
I'm here at last
I knock at the door
I plead, I ask

What do you hold
There, of my past
That I need today
So that I can now pass

Unto my next phase
And then to become
The next version of me
The process begun

Just B

Deep, Still Waters

Still waters run deep
We know this as a fact
When born sign of Scorpio
Life's mysteries come back

Intrigue it is found
As I move through the mist
To rituals that I feel
Still bound deep in my head

Searching day into night
For the elixir of life
To quench my great thirst
For what awaits after light

My lifetime of searching
Has moved me straight ahead
Over high mountains
While I lie deep in my bed

My dreams they reveal
Great stories untold
Of tales before time
When I was wise and old

Just B

My thirst it's still with me
I know not how to stop
All my delving and scrying
To be set free I adopt

A life full of joy
Synchronicities will be found
To help quench my great thirst
That's so deep and so profound

When my memories come calling
It is me who will ask
How do I move forward
And be whole at last?

Just B

The 3 The 6 and The 9

The power of the 3
The 6 and the 9
I know not what they mean
But I feel they're Divine

I ponder and think
About what they can do
In my unique lifetime
They will manifest too

Into something quite special
I know not just yet
What they will enlighten in me
I forget

The power of past lifetimes
Resides with them too
Together they guide me
And show me what to do

Just B

Dreamtime

My guides, my angels
My ancestors too
I greet them upon rising
And in nighttime too

They're the ones who are with me
All throughout the day
To teach and to guide me
In their own special way

Wherever I go
And whatever I say
It's my spiritual family
Who is leading my way

The night it is setting
There is still much to do
But as I head into Dreamtime
They will be there too

To guide and to lead me
Into my own dreamland
To decipher the meaning
I receive for The Plan

Just B

My Spiritual Masters
They are always the ones
To guide me and teach me
Just how to have fun

On my own special journey
Through wonderful lands
In my own special way
I will learn how to stand

Just B

My Master Plan

The spark now grows inside of me
The joy, the love, The Plan
Magic's special mixture
I feel it in my hands

It's growing deep inside of me
It creates my Master Plan
To manifest all my desires
Right now I take a stand

Love and light and gratitude
All are here with me now
Growing deep within my heart
My magic now starts to glow

Just B

True Love

Attachment and need
Do not equal love
Now I understand

Release your thirst
And you will burst
Like a child playing in sand

Then into your life
You will receive
Magic in your hands

Love yourself first
To then receive
The Universal Plan

True love's at
Your fingertips
Release it, let it flow

Into your life
Bit by bit
It will overflow

Just B

Synchronicities

Synchronicities abound
Everywhere they are found
Interests of the past
Opportunities at last

Once in the groove
Of the way that it moves
Chance meetings they say
They are meant for today

When you open your mind
Other people will find
Your gifts and your talents
They will all be aligned

Just B

Death and Rebirth

Death and rebirth
The Scorpio way
Pluto rising
Double the play

Constantly changing
Perfecting my way
Who am I now?
What do I display?

Start at the bottom
Move up to the top
Constant change
That is not meant to stop

Who I will become
From one year to the next
No one can know
No one can guess

Just B

Treasures

Who are you deep within?
Listen and begin
Journey back to your Self
The source of inner wealth

Listen for the sound
So deep and so profound
The message that it holds
Is made of precious gold

Talk to your creator
Release all of your pain
Then listen for the sound
Deep within and you will gain

All the answers that you seek
Lie there dormant way down deep
They are there for you to find
All your treasures deep inside

Just B

Whispered Secrets

Synchronicities are with you
They are all around
Are you awake in your life?
Listen for the sounds

Of Mother Nature whispering
Her secrets in your ear
Of gentle breaths, of subtle touches
Light upon your hair

So stay awake and watch
As you go about your day
For subtle innuendos
That present amongst the fray

They whisper secrets that you need
To move along your path
So stay awake, and stay alert,
You know not where they're at

Just B

Sand Castles

I'm like the Little Dutch Boy
With my finger in the dam
The waves beyond are crashing
Waiting to hit the land

The force within those waves
It is hard to comprehend
When they role beyond the dyke
Ready to make a stand

My finger is out! The wave has broke!
Oh, the beauty in the sand
So unique and intricate
It was not hard to let it land

Where will this wave take me?
Who will join the surf and sand?
As I build my own sand castles
I will start to understand

Just B

Innuendos

The sound of the surf is calling me
As if it knows my name
Whispering sweet innuendos
Of what I am meant to say

The breeze is fluttering through the grass
Like whispers in the night
Sounds of silence mixed within
The mystery taking flight

Butterflies, nature's messengers
Flutter all around
They too can sense the secrets
I'm meant to hear as sound

And still the waves crash to the shore
My messengers of might
Their crashing sound that breaks the ground
I now can see the light

Just B

The Shore

Mighty waves
With great fury
As they crash
To the shore

Leave you standing
Like a child
Wildly laughing
Wanting more

Soft golden sand
Underfoot
And in between
Your toes

Nature's carpet
Soft and gentle
Greets the waves
On the shore

Nature's call
So sublime
Thanks to you
For being mine

Just B

Alchemy

Take a peek
You will see
Joy playing
With ecstasy

Look again
To comprehend
Love's need
To run again

The three unite
In a field of light
The alchemy
Is pure delight

Just B

Butterfly

Wondrous transformers
Where do you fly?
Day by day
Up in the great sky

What purpose you hold
Flying there in plain sight
What places you journey to
On your great plight

Your fragile wings
Hold you up in the air
And carry you forward
To your new affair

To strengthen your journey
You travel afar
To whatever awaits you
You are my North Star

Just B

Delicate Creatures

I used to see just a butterfly
Flying ahead of me
Now I see two, sometimes three
Many now flutter all around me

Beautiful messengers from nature
That bountiful Mother called Earth
Whose treasures that fly all around me
Are priceless wherever they be

I love these delicate creatures
They are truly gifts to me
Thank you oh powerful Gaia
For sending them to visit me

Just B

Gaia's Call

Are you awake
Or still fast asleep?
Do you feel Mother Earth
Grounding your feet?

As you tread on Her land
Do you know, understand?
Can you open your eyes
And see where you stand?

She is calling to you
You must help as you can
Powerful Gaia she needs you
Please lend her a hand

Just B

Moon so Bright

The sound of surf
The moon so bright
Shining down
Its magnificent light

Magnificent light
What splendor there
You make me want
To stop and stare

You light the sky
For me to see
Give me a sign
Of who to be

You are my guide
So strong and true
You show me what
I am to do

Just B

The New Me

I have
Places to go
People to see
Things to do
To be the new me

Out of the shadows
I slowly creep
Into the spotlight
Like a meek little sheep

I know not what I'm doing
Or where this might go
I release all my fears
To move forward and grow

I rely on my faith
In my guides leading me
To the next phase of my life
To be the new me

Just B

The Circle of Giving

My gifts that await me
They are yet to be told
They're my guideposts to measure
My path that unfolds

Moving steadily forward
To the next phase of my plan
I still wonder what purpose
My next venture will have

I will trust in my guides
They know what I still need
To experience in this life
And help others believe

In their own special uniqueness
And their purpose to hold
Their own special encounters
That help others unfold

Just B

Setting Sail

Freedom is upon me
I feel it coming fast
Vancouver on the horizon
I will be there at long last

Old East Coast Soul
From days of old
Is where my life
Was cast

My sail is set
I'm moving west
To break
The Iron Mask

I set my sail
I will prevail
I'm heading west
At last

Just B

Miracle

Ride the wave
Go with the flow
How long it will last
No one can know

Relax and enjoy
Each day as it comes
Moments we share
When we truly care

Precious encounters
Rare and unique
Believe in a miracle
The one you seek

Just B

My Plan

My plan right now
Is to simply believe
I will follow the messages
That I receive

What that entails
Will soon be revealed
As I listen to my guides
My plan will be sealed

My path is perfect
In every way
To live all the blessings
That are coming my way

Just B

Freedom

My gift of words received late in life
Are the release valve
For all of my pain
I have suppressed throughout my life

What a wonderful gift
A creative fix
For all of my past troubles to flow out of me
To heal me and whoever else feels them

I am no longer under cover
Hiding from myself or from anyone else
This is me, I accept and love me
Finally I Am FREE

Just B

I See the Light

Do you believe in a Universe
full of kindness and love?
One that is benevolent
and forgiving?

I now do.
And what a beautiful realization it is.
My new perspective has taken
a weight off of me.
My spirit is free to lead me to wonderful
new creations that I cannot even begin to imagine.

I simply have to release my negativity, my pain,
and forgive all in my life that has hurt me.
For I have brought it all into my reality,
and I will release it, to embrace
my new existence of abundance,
with gratitude and love.

Thank You, Creator for letting me see the Light!

Just B

Precious Gift

Soul bared
Standing naked on this earth
To my first poem
I did give birth

The words started to trickle
Into my head
The first two lines
The rest I was fed

The birth of this poem
My precious third child
I will nurture and cherish
I will chisel as mine

So unexpected
So out of the blue
What was coming?
No one knew

Magic and splendor
Has touched down in me
My own creative
Individuality

Just B

To share with the world
What to do with my gift?
My path will unfold
As my soul bequests

Just B

Journey Home

I have finished this journey
I'm onto my next
What adventures await me
On my next cosmic quest

This lifetime's travels
So wondrous and true
Are but my stepping stones
To my next rendezvous

So into the mystic
I venture with glee
Knowing my angels
Are there leading me

What wonders and treasures
Await my next quest
As I journey towards
My next lifetime's best

Don't cry for my loss
Please rejoice, I am free
I have left this incarnation
To be the true me

Just B

Prayer to My Goddess

Oh my Goddess
Strong and true
Hear me today
Show me what to do

Always with me
Leading my way
Show me what I
Must do today

Forging forward
Towards my goals
Keep them strong
Made out of gold

Just B

CPSIA information can be obtained
at www.ICGtesting.com
Printed in the USA
LVHW051910110619
620905LV00001B/1